# PLANTING
# SEEDS

written by Amy Jo

illustrated by Dorothy Donohue

**McGraw-Hill
School Division**

New York            Farmington

He is planting bean seeds.

She is planting carrot seeds.

He is planting pumpkin seeds.

4

She is planting corn seeds.

He is planting tomato seeds.

She is planting beet seeds.

They have a garden of colors.